I Talk about It
All the Time

I Talk about It
All the Time

CAMARA LUNDESTAD JOOF

Translated by Olivia Noble Gunn

THE UNIVERSITY OF WISCONSIN PRESS

Supported by the Society for the Advancement of Scandinavian Study and the Sverre Arestad Endowed Chair in Norwegian Studies at the University of Washington, Seattle.

The University of Wisconsin Press
728 State Street, Suite 443
uwpress.wisc.edu

Printed in the United States of America
This book may be available in a digital edition.

Library of Congress Cataloging-in-Publication Data

Names: Joof, Camara Lundestad, 1988– author. | Gunn, Olivia Noble, translator.
Title: I talk about it all the time / Camara Lundestad Joof.
Other titles: Eg snakkar om det heile tida. English
Description: Madison, Wisconsin : The University of Wisconsin Press, [2024]
Identifiers: LCCN 2023043893 | ISBN 9780299348540 (paperback)
Subjects: LCSH: Joof, Camara Lundestad, 1988– | Racially mixed people—Norway—Biography. | Race discrimination—Norway. | LCGFT: Autobiographies.
Classification: LCC DL537.J66 A3 2024 | DDC 305.8/05966610481092 [B]—dc23/eng/20240220
LC record available at https://lccn.loc.gov/2023043893

Your silence will not protect you.

—AUDRE LORDE

Contents

ix

Introduction

Let's Talk about Race

MONICA L. MILLER and NANA OSEI-KOFI

When the killing of children is the measure of whether an act is racist or not, when this is where the line is drawn, racism is effectively disappeared.

We are having a conversation with Camara Lundestad Joof and Olivia Noble Gunn about this book as Joof shares with us the ways in which her stories are about the small things, microaggressions, experiences of coincidence, of chance, and the repetition of acts of racism as part of the everyday, in addition to the occasional and extreme. One of the things we learn from her is that, apart from content on two racist acts in contemporary Norwegian history that resulted in the death of young people of color, when *I Talk about It All the Time* was published in 2018, it became the first text used in Norwegian schools to discuss race and racism as matters that are about more than singular, extreme acts of violence.

As we reflected on the aforementioned as part of our discussion about writing this introduction, we grappled with the question of how we might help explain how race functions in Norway to readers in the United States. While potentially extreme to an American audience, Joof's statement about the killing of children powerfully captures how racism has historically been viewed by Norwegian society. As a way of speaking to some of the many complex layers of this conceptualization of race and racism, we offer our conversation with Joof and our subsequent conversation with each other as an invitation to you, the reader, to bear witness to the small things as well as the large and structural concepts that make up the meaning of Blackness and anti-Blackness specifically, and of race and racism more broadly, in Norway.

At the time of writing *I Talk about It All the Time*, Joof was well known as a hip-hop artist, playwright, and performer, having had great success with her theatrical debut, the autobiographical performance *Pavlov's Bitch* in 2015. The daughter of a white Norwegian woman and a Gambian father, an immigrant to Norway from Banjul, Camara grew up in Sandefjord, Norway. Combining stand-up comedy, music, and stories, her work centers on how she navigates Norwegian society as a biracial/Black, queer young woman, about which she notes the following in a recent interview: "Whether or not you want to be political, it becomes political when a black woman is on stage. . . . If you do not want something to be political any longer, then you must work with it politically. . . . You cannot avoid it."[1] As such, Joof describes this book as written both for the readers who might recognize themselves in the text, who identify with the "I" of the text, as well as for those to whom she directs her efforts at creating awareness and recognition of how race works in Norway, that is to say, the "you" to whom she also writes (more on this later). Hence, our exchange on the pages that follow necessarily began with the need to say something about who we are and how we enter into this dialogue.

MONICA: As an African American woman who is also a scholar of African American and African diasporic literature and cultural studies, I have always been interested in what Ashon Crawley has called the "otherwise possibilities" of Blackness, the idea that Blackness can and should be defined expansively and not exclusively around known trajectories, geographies, or notions of authenticity.[2] What Joof teaches me is a continuation of this lesson that I have been learning since I began studying African Scandinavian cultural production more than a decade ago. I come to African Scandinavian studies through my curiosity and concern about how race and Blackness are conceptualized and lived in Sweden, thinking in particular about my own African American / Swedish children and their futures, wherever they chose to live and call home. For me, Joof's memoir captures so much of what I have observed and am still learning about the lived experience of race, racism, and Blackness in Scandinavia: the weight of the silence; the isolation from and difficulty of forming Black-identified or race-conscious community; the exhausting repetition of everyday racism; the enduring need for one's experiences of the silencing, isolation, and repetition to be acknowledged and for the conversation about "it" to begin again from a different place.

NANA: To me, the question of who I am and how I enter a conversation is a question that is about meaning making and what is useful for someone to know about me as a human being and a scholar as they engage with my work. To this point, our dialogue about Joof's text is a conversation that I enter as an African Swedish feminist scholar based in the United States. I was born in Sweden to a Ghanaian father and a Swedish mother, more than twenty years before Joof, and yet I see my younger self in many of the fragments and stories that she shares about growing up and experiencing young adulthood as a Black woman in Norway. As a scholar, I am committed to engaging in work that can contribute to social change, and through which complex social relations that create and perpetuate social and economic injustice can be more deeply understood and challenged, which is something I also recognize in Joof's work. I have spent several decades engaged in intersectional feminist scholarship in the United States, while maintaining ties to Sweden and Scandinavia, and it is through this lens—of both political commitments and social location—alongside my current work, which focuses on Black identity in Sweden, that I engage with what I would argue has been our key question in reading this work: what is critical for an American or English-language reader to understand about race in Norway in order to fully engage with the experiences that Joof brings to life through her storytelling?

MONICA: *I Talk about It All the Time* offers lessons different from but related to American and African American history and life. Joof's memoir presents the possibility for (un)learning what we think we know about how race, racialization, and racism work as well as, most importantly and generously, not only how these concepts are lived but how they feel. Many African Americans and other Americans understand a great deal about race, racism, racialization, and Blackness, given their shared history of slavery, abolition/Reconstruction, Jim Crow, and the civil rights and Black Power movements. Sometimes they feel like they know everything there is to know. Too often African American models of race and conceptions of Blackness are thought to be applicable to the whole world, despite the fact that histories of racialization, colonization, and imperialism change the forms that Blackness and anti-Blackness take globally, which makes the question that has shaped this introduction such an important one.

NANA: Indeed. When I first read Joof's text, it made me think about the interplay between microaggressions and macro-aggressions (concepts developed in the United States) and about the inability of Norwegian society to recognize how constant and repeated microaggressions stem from structural racism perpetrated against people of color. What I quickly recognized, however, was that in ways similar to Sweden, in the Norwegian context, you can't simply say that microaggressions are in fact racist acts; by doing so, you run the risk of not being believed or being dismissed through tokenization. As Joof mentioned in our conversation, her book is as much a discussion of *how* to talk about race as it is a conversation *about* race. The word *racism* is only mentioned a half-dozen times in the text, as she describes wanting her readers to come to this realization for themselves, to recognize that experience, after experience, after experience, can't simply be dismissed as coincidence. And I must say, this pedagogical choice, while unquestionably frustrating to anyone who knows the experience of racism and/or to whom the existence of racism is obvious, seems to have worked in the way Joof as educator intended, as early discussions of the book by white readers when it first came out in Norway used language like "an eyeopener" and "a punch to the gut" to describe the impact of the content of the book.[3] At the same time, she told us that she heard from teenage boys of color that *I Talk about It All the Time* was the first and only book they had ever read from cover to cover.

MONICA: Just as Joof's work is distinctly Norwegian, at the same time it is also related to African American history and scholarship. Her work is an illustration of the ways in which the work of many African Scandinavian artists, in particular those of Joof's generation and older, is heavily influenced by African

American and other writers and thinkers working in English, as these were the only texts they had access to that had a vocabulary to describe racism, racialization, and racial consciousness. For example, Joof chose a quotation from scholar Audre Lorde, who self-described as a "black, lesbian, feminist, mother, warrior, poet," as the epigraph to *I Talk about It All the Time*, and I see so many writers of color and their texts, both older and contemporary, echoing in Joof's own: for example, Claudia Rankine's *Citizen: An American Lyric* (which Joof co-translated with Kristina Leganger Iversen around the same time she wrote this book), Audre Lorde's *Zami: A New Spelling of My Name*, and Sara Ahmed's feminist killjoy from *Willful Subjects*.[4] I even see Toni Morrison here, especially in how this book is framed. Morrison famously said that her books are difficult because the history of race and Blackness in the United States has not been easy. Similarly, Joof does not let readers off easily, and at the same time, she is working very hard to provide all her readers with the tools they need to work through their experiences with racialization and racism.

Related to this, when reading *I Talk about It All the Time* and in our conversation with Joof, I was continually struck by her frustration about being an educator and the unrelenting need for her to fulfill this role, no matter how painful the "lesson" is to herself and others. In "Quitting," she laments, "I regularly decide to quit talking to white people about racism. Sometimes because it feels like wasted energy, an unproductive encounter with their feelings of guilt. . . . Because I pay an enormous emotional price for having these conversations again and again" (5).

NANA: What I think of as the pedagogical as a focus and specifically how Joof experiences this in her body also had an impact on me. The seeming pressure to educate, the resentment of the need to do so, of the expectation from a white majority, and at the same time the reluctant desire to tell her story, to bring about change, maybe, just maybe, is in many ways a defining element of Joof's text. Filled with doubt, Joof shares a range of feelings that will be familiar to those who know what it feels like to be Black in a white world. They are the feelings that Lorde wrote about in *Sister Outsider* when she referenced the ways in which we as "Black and Third World people are expected to educate white people as to our humanity."[5] Feelings often carry with them a heightened sense of anger and frustration for people of color in Scandinavia, wherein a willful ignorance continues to forcefully place the existence of racialization and racism in question. At the same time, what is noteworthy is the sophistication with which Joof takes up the question of always being expected to show up as the pedagogue. In the fragments of her experiences that she details throughout the book, her sense of doubt and frustration is palpable. These are moments in which Joof does not have full control, where she must decide what she will or will not do at every juncture. Concomitantly, the very act of compiling these moments into the short, accessible, pedagogical text that is *I Talk about It All the Time* is an act through which she owns her power. She is making a choice to speak, demanding to be heard by a white majority, and offering what Olivia Noble Gunn, in the translator's note to this book, describes as both a gift and a challenge.

> So, at this point, as a reader, you may be wondering
> how this text came into being.

Just as she does not want to educate all the time, Joof also did not really want to write this book. In our conversation with her, we learned how and why she wrote this text, some of which was surprising. She did not write so "willingly." Instead, she was asked to write a short book that would be part of a series called Norwegian Truth, which was designed to recruit more diverse voices into Norwegian literature. The series prioritized accessibility and was targeted to Norwegian youth. Each book had to be written in Nynorsk (New Norwegian), the much less used of two official written languages in Norway; be fewer than one hundred pages; accessible; pedagogical; and readable in an hour.

In terms of how the text is composed, Joof wrote all the pieces and then placed them on the floor—she and her editor then sequenced them, thinking about how to build trust with a reader even though the text is full of moments in which Joof wonders if she accesses her own memories with accuracy and transparency. Though the content is heavy, the fragmentary form gives readers time and space to sit with Joof's experiences. Readers can read and ponder these fragments one by one, as part of a cycle in the book, or as they accumulate. Even when told and read in fragments, the moments of sexual exploitation and extreme physical violence are almost too much to bear; their accumulation into this book, their pacing, and their placement all enable Joof to survive the narration of these stories and her readers to absorb them without being completely overwhelmed.

Though the pieces are written as if Joof is speaking directly to the reader, they are addressed to different "you's": Black and white, family, friends, lovers, and strangers. This multiplicity of address was designed to engage all readers and to allow them, regardless of their race, to see themselves in this book. Since Joof began her career as a performer and playwright, this active nature of the text was very important, as the book unfolds in "scenes." Joof and her editor were also careful not to "hit" the reader with one of the more or most violent episodes early, so that Norwegian readers in particular would not understand "racism" as only that which is spectacular and physically violent. As she explains in the text, Joof was insistent that she not be seen as a victim or even a complainer. Instead, the pacing of the incidents and the echoes across the entire book had to paint a clear-eyed portrait of a person who has experienced all of this and remains reliable, despite the fact that racism has profoundly affected her life and sense of who she is in the world. In an interview about the book, Joof describes what appears essential to her ability to share her experiences in ways that are at once personal, political, and pedagogical. She is adamant about never putting anything before an audience that she herself hasn't first worked through in therapy, noting that she won't ever use art as therapy or the audience as therapist.[6] We also learned that this isn't just an aesthetic concern but a legal one. In Norway, authors of nonfiction books have legal responsibility for what they write and could be asked to "prove" that what they write is true. For this reason, Joof was very intentional about what she included and how, and she mused metatextually about the politics of what she included. Although readers might see themselves in episodes of Joof's book, it was important to her that the book is her story and her story alone, and that people could see that these experiences can happen to one person.

NANA: In all these ways, Joof's text is a clear and unapologetic engagement with the politics of race, not only in Norway but throughout African Scandinavia, as she includes fragments of experiences in Sweden and Denmark in the text. Among the stories she tells, she describes feeling a sense of freedom from being racialized while in Sweden. The person with whom she is in conversation, a man who is a friend, flippantly attributes this sense of freedom to Swedish political correctness and to Swedes' fear of verbalizing what they truly think. As a result, Joof speculates about the meaning of a certain directness that is attributed to Norway and Denmark, and at the same time she finds some relief in the hesitancy that the notion of political correctness brings into being, a slight discomfort and fear to express thoughts and feelings about her body, her being. Illustrating the seeming directness of encounters in Denmark, she recounts how drunk Danes who ask her about where she is from have seemingly nothing to say about her brown skin as long as she doesn't seek to lay claim to Danishness. There is the story of a taxi driver in Copenhagen engaging in a line of questioning related to his long-held desire to have sex with a Black woman; the slap on her behind by a man who is a stranger to her, while locking up her bike in central Copenhagen; and the teacher who in passing uneventfully calls her *neger*, during what is supposed to be a collegial group conversation over dinner.

What Joof's work illustrates is that while there may be slight variations in the ways in which race may be taken up in different Scandinavian countries, discourses on race in Scandinavia, regardless of the country in which they take place, are essentially informed by a Scandinavian exceptionalism that rests on the idea that these discourses have no place in Scandinavia and that this region of the world is supposedly made up of nations for which processes and practices of racialization are completely absent, and where equity and justice reign supreme.[7] For these reasons, Joof's work, which so clearly shatters this myth, had wide-reaching impact on discourses on race in Norway when it was first published, and it continues to be an important contribution to conversations on race in Scandinavia. As one of the first texts in Norwegian to take up these issues, it created a foundation on which others could and have built. No longer does taking up racialization in Norway mean that writers must start with the most foundational of concepts and theories. In these ways, Joof's work also occupies an important place in Black European studies as it gives voice to both the specificity of the African Scandinavian experience and some of the many similarities with which race is taken up throughout Europe.

MONICA: The sense that a foundation is being built for these conversations all over Scandinavia is important and so true. There has been an explosion of memoir and autobiographical literature and theater by African Scandinavian artists in the past few years. In the case of Sweden, I'm thinking of Jason "Timbuktu" Diakité's *En Droppe Midnatt* (2018) (translated into English as *A Drop of Midnight* in 2020; also adapted for performance in Swedish and English), and in Finland, Koko Hubara's *Ruskeat Tytöt* (Brown girls) (2017).[8] We might think of the *I Am Queen Mary* sculpture project by African Danish artist Jeanette Ehlers and African Caribbean artist La Vaughn Bell in a similar way—though not autobiographical, the sculpture does use the fused likenesses of the artists to depict the rebelling labor activist Queen Mary as a way to talk about the shared history of slavery and imperialism between Denmark and the Danish West Indies / US Virgin Islands. Like Joof, these writers and artists all share the urge to tell stories about surviving the overwhelming whiteness of Scandinavia, and they describe the ways in which they feel gaslighted by notions of colorblindness and Nordic exceptionality; they are also all dedicated to detailing how creativity and art enable this survival.

Can we change society by witnessing? . . .
How many stories do we need? How many stories is enough?

At the end of *I Talk about It All the Time*, Joof meditates on the importance of witnesses—she desperately needs and wants corroboration of her story about the racism she faces, the difficulties and ironies of being "brown first" in Norway. If you are reading this book, you hold Joof's story in your hands; you are carrying a story of survival. Joof's experiences and the stories she tells about being brown in Norway are now your memories of reading *I Talk about It All the Time*: the physical book and its readers have become witnesses and hopefully anti-racist activists and allies. In writing this book, Joof took responsibility for addressing the racism she experienced (and initially ignored in the case of her brother and other Black and brown folx), while leaving other responsibilities to us: the difficult but necessary task of doing our own work of recognizing and fighting everyday and structural racism.

Notes

1. Birgitta Haglund, "En bitch som söker dialog," *Teatertidningen* 3 (2016), https://teatertidningen.se/?p=1327.
2. See Ashon Crawley, *Blackpentecostal Breath: The Aesthetics of Possibility* (New York: Fordham University Press, 2016).
3. "Eg snakkar om det heile tida," Bibliotekets literaturpris, podcast, July 2022, https://www.biblioteketslitteraturpris.no/eg-snakkar-om-det-heile-tida-2018/.
4. Alexis De Veaux, *Warrior Poet: A Biography of Audre Lorde* (New York: W. W. Norton, 2004), 179; Claudia Rankine, *Citizen: An American Lyric* (New York: Dramatists Play Service, 2018); Claudia Rankine, *Medborgar eit amerikansk dikt* (Oslo: Samlaget, 2018); Audre Lorde, *Zami: A New Spelling of My Name* (Berkeley: Crossing Press, 1982); Sara Ahmed, *Willful Subjects* (Durham, NC: Duke University Press, 2014).
5. Audre Lorde, *Sister Outsider: Essays and Speeches* (Berkeley: Crossing Press, 1984), 115.

6. "Hør her'a: Eg snakkar om det heile tida," Camara Lundestad Joof og Gulariz Sharif i samtale med Ida Vågsether, Jakob Sande-senter for forteljekunst, March 10, 2021, https://www.youtube.com/watch?v=LFe xopiTI4Y.

7. Lena Sawyer and Ylva Habel, eds., "Refracting African and Black Diaspora through the Nordic Region," special issue, *African and Black Diaspora: An International Journal* 7, no. 1 (2014).

8. Jason Timbuktu Diakité, *En Droppe Midnatt* (Stockholm: Vilja förlag, 2018); Jason Timbuktu Diakité, *A Drop of Midnight: A Memoir*, trans. Rachel Willson-Broyles (Seattle: Amazon Crossing, 2020); Koko Hubara, *Ruskeat Tytöt* (Helsinki: Like, 2017).

I Talk about It
All the Time

Dear Brother,

Throughout our childhood, the white side of our family called us negerbarna, *the negro children. It was said playfully and affectionately, with love. Our cousins and second cousins got to be the children of this or that uncle or aunt, but we were always mom's* negerbarn.

The chocolate children.

And I remember when I was eleven.

I remember that your whole body shook. You trembled. It was Grandma's birthday, and you tried to explain to all the adults at once that you didn't want to deal with it anymore. You couldn't stand that word. That word made your body recoil. It was wrong. It hurt. Blinking back tears, your voice increased in volume, and you were clumsy and inarticulate, too angry to be clear.

And you were thirteen.

And then you were told that this is the way it's always been, and that's the way it will always be. We've always used that word. People also call those chocolate pastries negerbollar. *Is everything we do suddenly wrong, now? Oh my god, you've grown up in Norway, not in the United States. You're being very sensitive, dear. We don't mean any harm by it.*

And then Grandma turned to me and said:

Camara doesn't have a problem with us using that word. Right . . . ?

And I answered that I didn't have a problem with it.

That I actually liked it. That we do say negerbollar *in this country, after all. And that you were ridiculous if you thought you were a gangster from the USA.*

Because when I agreed with the adults, they liked me better. And that was more important than if you liked me. Because I thought you were a jerk.

And you deflated like a balloon. You didn't pop. You must have understood that you were on your own. You went out in the backyard and sat down. The adults said I should let you finish sulking in peace. I stayed inside and ate banana cake. It felt like I had won something.

My body hadn't recoiled. Not yet.

I dream about it at night.

We've never talked about this, you and me. And I've never apologized. But I promise I will before this book goes to print.

Quitting

I often decide to quit. I regularly decide to quit talking to white people about racism. Sometimes because it feels like wasted energy, an unproductive encounter with their feelings of guilt. The guilt often manifests in tears. Sometimes I feel like I'm getting paid to make people cry.

Sometimes I decide to quit when I encounter the entrenched defensiveness that whiteness assumes when it's reminded that it's white.

Nobody likes to be reminded of their skin color. Some people get really angry.

And anything I have to say could be said almost as clearly by other white people, and it wouldn't cost them so much to say it. And maybe people would be more willing to listen to them.

Because I pay an enormous emotional price for having these conversations again and again. It's emotional labor. I enter into all these conversations in a kind of educator mode. There is no such thing as a dumb question, I say. I take a deep breath and answer, and the educator doesn't abandon me. In the end, it gets hard to turn her off.

So, when I'm sitting in a taxi in Copenhagen and the driver asks where I come from and what I do, I answer. And when he asks what kind of art I make, I answer. And when he asks if he can ask me a personal question, I say yes. And then he asks me if I think there's a difference racially between Black women and white women when it comes to sex. He has always wanted to sleep with a Black woman because there might be something more animalistic about us, in our DNA in a way. Or do I think it might have more to do with culture than skin color? Then I answer him. And the educator is activated. So I answer matter-of-factly. And slowly. In plain words, without noise, speaking in a calm voice. And he thanks me for my answer and says he hadn't thought about that. That he'll think more about it. And maybe next time he'll even think better of it. I pay and get out of the taxi. I smoke a cigarette before I ring the bell at my friend's place. Because I don't want to be the one who comes storming into the apartment for a visit and makes everything about me and whatever just happened to me. This happened to me, a person who once again makes everything about herself and the color of her skin. So, I smoke a cigarette before I ring up. I pull the smoke deep into my lungs, draw it down into my belly.

What's in a Name?

I debate with myself: which name should I use for this book?

My name is Camara Christina Lundestad Joof.

Camara Joof is a more compelling name than Camara Lundestad Joof. I can just forget about Christina—it's way too long—even though it's important to me because there are three generations of women on my maternal grandma's side with the middle name Christina. Always the firstborn daughter. I'm the firstborn daughter.

There are seven of us siblings. I have two siblings, two stepsiblings, and two half-siblings. We are three full siblings then, when I count myself. And of the three of us, I'm the only one christened Lundestad. Everyone else just got the name Joof. And I've always felt that meant I took after mom more than they did. That I got to belong to her family a bit more.

I moved to Oslo when I was eighteen. My first job was as a telephone salesperson. On the first day of work, I was told to introduce myself as Christina Lundestad when I made calls. My group manager said it invited trust, and it would be to my benefit because I worked on commission. It didn't occur to me to protest.

I remember I thought it was probably smart, that I should have thought of that myself.

I've always been interested in asserting myself, showing that I belong, impressing people with my Norwegian dialects. I was born here. Look at my passport, it says place of birth Bodø, not birthplace unknown. Don't just look at my passport, listen to my name. Believe me.

After I moved to Oslo, I was careful not to sit next to people on the tram, subway, or bus who have, as we say in Norway, visible immigrant backgrounds. For the first three years, I never sat by another brown person because I was terrified other passengers on the bus would think we were in a gang.

I use Camara Joof when I put out music. Sometimes just Camara. Then my voice can carry everything. And, honestly, it's actually an advantage because I mostly work in hip-hop. Unlike all those white men who hop around, I don't need to give myself a dope stage name with numbers in it to seem authentic. I get my cred for free.

But when I'm writing? In these political identity projects of mine? Then Lundestad quashes a good deal of debate before it even begins, and I hide behind it. I share a name with the man who was responsible for the Nobel Prize. Fuck you and your questions.

I've spent a lot of time insisting on my Norwegianness, defending my right to belong, proving I own it, just as much as I own the right to wear what I want, where I want.

When people ask me where I come from, I willfully misunderstand them. I tell them Sandefjord. And when they ask where I *really* come from, I answer Bodø. I was born in Bodø. And I say it in a thick Norwegian dialect. Then, when they shake their heads and say, oh, no, but where . . . I respond:

Oh, are you wondering why I'm brown?
And the discomfort is palpable.
No, no, it wasn't that . . .
Yes, I insist, you're wondering why I'm brown. If that's not what you were thinking about, then the answer I gave you earlier would have been enough. You would have accepted both answers. I am brown because my father was born in Banjul, Gambia. And my mother was born in Mosjøen, Norway.

I make it difficult because I think it's difficult to get the same question over and over again. It feels like I have the same conversations over and over again. I talk about the same things all the time.

Like other Norwegian tourists in Thailand, I get stopped by children running in the street when I travel out to country villages. These children have never seen hair like mine, or they're fascinated by the color of my skin. And it doesn't bother me either. Because I don't live in Thailand. I'm not from there. Those children are allowed to touch my hair. You are not.
At home the question makes me uncomfortable because I have to insist that I belong here. And I'm uncomfortable because I sometimes doubt that I really do.
I'm uncomfortable, but I've decided that I don't have a problem answering, as long as we can be uncomfortable together. I'm just obstinate enough to refuse to carry the discomfort alone. If you want to know where I come from, then you get to carry the discomfort too. Own what you are really asking about.

But not in Denmark. I lived in Copenhagen for four years, and in Denmark I think it's brilliant when drunk people ask where I come from. You aren't Danish, are you?
No, I answer, I'm Norwegian.

And as long as I don't dare to claim Danishness, most often it's all the fucking same to them whether or not I'm Norwegian, and usually within ten minutes someone throws the oil fund in my face.

Jer og jeres fucking olje. You and your fucking oil.

And yes. It's my oil. In Denmark, I own all the Norwegian oil. And I become an obnoxious Norwegian who rubs it in, who says that I have a little oil well in my garden, just like all the other Norwegians, and a little well at the cabin, like all the other Norwegians, and I go to the backyard and pump up a mug of oil from my well and go to the Kiwi grocery store chain and buy Norwegian brown cheese with it. And all the most famous Norwegians, like Petter Northug. And Sissel Kyrkjebø. And Cecilia Brækhus. And Bjørn Dæhlie.

I'm so Norwegian that when I was little, a friend and I sold small figurines made of pine cones for ten øre in the street. And the ten-øre coin had gone out of production, so people had to give us fifty øre. And on our display table, with the pine-cone figurines and flowers we had stolen from the neighbor's garden, there was a sign that read, "Proceeds go to hungry children in Africa and to Norway's great Olympic hope, skier Bjørn Dæhlie."

A man came over and asked to buy two figurines for one Norwegian crown. But he said he'd rather the money just go to us, or to all the hungry children in Africa, because Bjørn Dæhlie didn't need help, he already had enough. And then I told him we wouldn't sell him anything because he had bad-mouthed Bjørn Dæhlie, and that simply wasn't done.

That's how Norwegian I am. But I'm not white. And that's why this book will be published under the name Camara Lundestad

Joof. I'll keep Lundestad, even though it isn't ideal, phonetically speaking. I've decided that this is OK as long as I'm clear with myself about why I'm doing it.

That's what it's like when you use art as a tool. There's less room for aesthetics.

Friend First

I think a lot about what people talk about when I'm not around. Do white people spend a lot of time discussing the N-word? Do they sit in cafés, bars, during lunch, at work, day in and day out, talking about it? About its history and usage and whether or not it's OK to say it? Do they ask white strangers what they think? Do they say to other white people they don't know, I've thought this and I've thought about that . . . and I wonder if you think it's racist? Can you spare a minute?

Most of my friends are white. I live in Scandinavia. Most of the people around me are white. It often occurs to me that I spend a disproportionate amount of my time talking about racism. Being asked about racism. Being sent links about racism. Inspiring articles, hysterical memes. My Facebook feed overflows with them. Mark Zuckerberg's algorithms have created an echo chamber just for me. And I often wonder if the people I know send these links to other people they know. In order to say, This is important. Or do they only send them to me? Do they only discuss the word *neger* when I'm there, or do they sit among themselves discussing it too?

This thought makes me happy. I think, Maybe the engagement goes deep enough that I'm not a trigger in the room, a catalyst for talking about a difficult subject. I try to avoid bringing it up. I bring it up all the time. It always comes up. Before I meet my friends, I plan out what I'm going to talk about. How much have I talked about racism this week? Or the last time we got a beer? How much have I talked about things that happened to me? Things that happened to other people?

I'm a witness to the truth. I'm a political project. I'm brown. But I'm a friend first. First, I want to be one of the people around the table who balances the conversation out. We talk a little bit about me, we talk a little bit about you, we talk a little bit about us. But when I'm there, when my skin color is there, it's hard to change the subject back to you afterward. It's difficult for you, maybe because you don't want to appear disrespectful. It's hard for me, too. I get all wrapped up in it. I can't bring myself to drop it. I need you to believe me. I'd rather let it go. It's just that once I get started, I become monomaniacal. Anal. I become brown first, friend second.

Sometimes I feel relieved when I get called nigger in front of a person I know. I think, There, now you witnessed it. The next time it comes up, *you* can tell the story. *You* can go to the café the following week with someone else and say it happened. This happened to you, too. So I can let it go.

And when I meet friends at the café two weeks later, and they ask how I'm doing, and I don't mention the time someone called me nigger at the emergency room, on Karl Johan, at Oslo City mall, in a bar, then they can say they know, they heard about what happened. And they can ask why I didn't say anything. And then I can say, well it wasn't anything out of the ordinary. It happens so often, all the time, I don't tell you every time it happens, even though it seems like I talk about it all the time. I talk about it all the time. And then they might think, Oh, she's brown first. And she's trying not to be. She's also a friend. It happened, it happens often, it happens more often than we realized. And then I can let it go. Because when I'm fixated, I'm not just brown first and a friend second. I make you all white first, too.

National Costume I

We have a national costume in our family, a children's *bunad* from Nordland County. It was embroidered by Inga Rørvik, one of three women who created the design. The Nordland *bunad* is the national costume most often awarded (unofficially) Norway's most beautiful. I'm not talking about the green version, but the blue coastal one, and that's important. Our children's *bunad* is passed down in the family to kids old enough to wear it. When I was six years old, it was my turn.

My maternal grandma is withdrawing money from the ATM. I'm standing in the square, and I'm glowing. I'm swishing my skirt. I'm not wearing the traditional bonnet. It's the 17th of May, Norway's constitution day. And two ladies—I remember them as ancient, at least one hundred years old—come over to me to say something about my dress. So, you're wearing a *bunad* from Nordland, are you? Yes, I say, and explain that it's always been in my family, that when a person is old enough, they get to wear it, and I'm old enough, because I'm turning seven years old in two weeks. And I spin around and pose. One of the ladies hits me on the arm with her umbrella. She tells me I have no business wearing this dress. It's disrespectful of me to wear it. You have no right, she says. And then I get another smack on the arm. I should be ashamed, standing there and openly bragging about something that isn't mine. I rub my arm and stare at her.

Then Grandma comes running over, swinging. She hits one of the ladies with her purse. She raises her fist threateningly and tells them to go to hell, shouts that *they* are the ones who should be ashamed. The ladies run away, and Grandma is a superhero. She is furious and passionate, and she dries my tears and takes me to the amusement park. And even though I'm not allowed to have sugar at home, she buys me two whole bags of cotton candy, and I eat both bags and get so sick that I throw up after a carousel ride. On the national costume.

The listener gets really uncomfortable when I tell this story, so much so that the atmosphere gets tense . . . until Grandma shows up and saves the day, and the puke hits the *bunad*. Hits this symbol that maybe doesn't mean so much after all. When the story is over, we sit there relieved. Shocked and in disbelief, but also with a feeling of amused relief.

We get to believe that we would have been Grandma in this story. We're all so grateful for Grandma. Because if Grandma exists, then we get to be her. And not those old ladies. Never the lady who hit me with the umbrella. But what about her friend? The one who said nothing? Her silence was just as impactful as the umbrella. To me.

But the truth is that Grandma only arrived later, after the ladies had left.

There's a line from hell at the ATM on the 17th of May. They didn't have Venmo in the 1990s. Grandma couldn't help not being there, just like I couldn't help standing there. And because I didn't say anything, she couldn't do anything. And the smack wasn't so hard, and it wasn't long before I stopped rubbing my arm and got distracted by the parade.

Still, when I was a teenager and started talking about what happened, I put Grandma in the story—almost from the very beginning. Because, without Grandma, the story is too much to bear. It's too much for the listener. And sometimes it's even too much for me.

And after all, it's just another thing that happened to me. The point of the story is to say, This happened to me. It happened when I was little. When I didn't have words to talk about it. I didn't have a language to explain it to anyone, so I didn't say anything. And as an adult, I'm angry. I'm angry on behalf of the girl in the *bunad*, and I want to tell you about it. It matters to me that you understand why I'm angry. But I don't want to be the one who dominates the conversation again with a story about something that happened to me. This happened to me, again making everything about me and the color of my skin. So, I turn it into a story about Grandma the superhero. Sometimes for your sake, but probably mostly for my own.

A Less Significant Event

An older lady wearing a fur collar gets on bus 46, in the direction of Ullerntoppen. We're in the Majorstua neighborhood. I'm sitting on the rear-facing double seat, right next to the doors. The lady thinks she put her bus pass in her purse, but it ends up on the floor. She sits down facing the front of the bus.

I wave at her, say hey, and point to the floor.

She stares straight ahead and grips her purse tightly. I turn toward the walkway, looking behind me to figure out what scared her. I don't see anything.

I lean out into the aisle and say, Excuse me, are you the one who . . . ?

She turns away from me, tightening her grip on her purse, her knuckles whitening.

I look behind me again, just to double-check. I don't see anything strange. The bus drives off; people are sitting in their seats. The traffic slowly makes its way up to Vinderen.

I stand up and pick up her bus pass, brushing off the slush from the floor. She's staring out the window. I tap her on the shoulder.

She flinches.

She stares at me.

I soften my voice, give her the warmest smile I can manage, and say, Excuse me, I think you dropped this. She stares at me, releases her grip on the purse, stretches her other hand out to me, takes her pass.

I sit down again.

Before she gets off the bus at Holmen, she comes over to me.

Excuse me, I just wanted to say thank you. You are so well mannered. Very civilized. Thank you.

I smile again and say, No worries. My spit crackles under my tongue.

I pat myself on the back for making this experience less scary for her.

It must be exhausting, I think, walking around your own city—a city that no longer looks like the one you moved to—and feeling afraid, all the time.

It's exhausting for both of us.

Whiteness

I often get called white.

When we were arguing as teenagers, my brother used to yell at me, You're so fucking white, you know. The other teenagers at the summer camp at the Center for Anti-racism used to say, You're mad white, you know; you're going to go far.

When people call me white as an adult, it's supposed to be a compliment: I talk white, people tell me. I think white. I have white interests.

A boss once told me he was a white African. He took such pleasure in music, deep down in his soul. He was simply a white African. I tried to tell him that there are actually a whole lot of white Africans. But he said he wasn't one of them; he was, you know, an authentic white African, on the inside. My mom tells me something similar: that she's blacker than me on the inside, that I'm the whitest of us all. She has lived in Africa, after all. I've only lived in Scandinavia.

In addition to writing and acting, I work as an artistic and political consultant for governmental agencies and institutions, in both Norway and Europe. I often get to hear that I'm so uplifting to work with because I understand diversity and integration, structural racism, postcolonialism, communication strategy, and marketing, but I'm also white, so they understand me.

I'm not white.

They say it was meant as a compliment.

I reply that I don't aspire to be white. Not anymore.

And I wonder if I can add a line item to my invoice, because I'm standing there providing voluntary services. I'm not there to teach them how to talk to brown people. Or sometimes I am. But I'm not there to teach them how to talk to me.

Still, I understand that language. I've used it myself, in fact. When I was a teenager, my motto was, I'm a white middle-class girl in disguise—a lamb in wolf's clothing, if you will.

Everyone in my friend group in middle school had a nickname. We called Hans Petter HP, sometimes just Hans. Karianne was Kariannemis. Ida was Idamis. I got the nickname Darkie Brown, pronounced *Bjuunshwarten*, just like Harald Eia would have said it in a Kari Bremnes sketch on the comedy show *Team Antonsen*.

I always answered when someone called me that, as if it were a completely normal name. I thought, That's how Norwegian I am, so Norwegian that I don't find it problematic. Now I'm not so sure who I was trying to convince, myself or them. Maybe that's not so important?

Quid Pro Quo

Three men are walking right behind me as I wander down Bog-stadveien, tipsy, in the dark. One of the men cracks a joke to the others. Maybe they think I can't hear them because I have head-phones on.

He says, Since all Black men go around attacking our Norwe-gian women, maybe it's time that we take one of theirs, quid pro quo like.

The others laugh.

I act like I can't hear them over the music.

It was probably a joke. It must have been a joke.

I pass up the turn onto Schultz's gate, where I live, and keep walking up to the Majorstua intersection.

I'm almost certain it was a joke. Just the same, I walk up to the intersection.

If I'd been totally certain it was a joke, I would have turned around and said something. I could have said, That's not funny.

But I'm not sure, so I pick up the pace, trying to disappear into the crowd of people waiting for the night bus before I turn around and walk home.

It must have been a joke.

Pavlov's Bicycle

I ride my bicycle in Copenhagen. I love to bike.

I can bike when and where I want to, and no one tells me I shouldn't bike home alone at night. I bike to see friends, from the city, to my job. I lock and unlock my bike every day. Most often several times a day. When I started biking, I locked and unlocked my bike with straight legs and a straight back. I locked my bike with my body at a ninety-degree angle, straight in and out.

One day, someone slapped me on the butt. I was so perplexed that I almost laughed. I jumped. I turned around confused, and a man in his forties, who had already walked a ways down the road, shouted at me in sneering Danish, Sorry, but that ass was just so tempting, I simply couldn't control myself.

I didn't say anything, just stared at him while he wandered further down the street. He didn't run away. He wasn't afraid of me.

The next time somebody slapped my butt, it was a gang of boys, and they got what was coming to them in return. Instead of high-fiving each other, they had to take off running, while yelling, telling me to calm down, because I was chasing after them and shouting, Shove it up your own ass.

The third time I was drunk, and the man who slapped me was so old, and I was so tired that I just rolled my eyes, got on my bike, and headed home.

I have locked and unlocked my bike almost every day for four years. I've been slapped on the butt three times. If you think about it from a statistical perspective, it's not a common problem.

I'm on a date. When I unlock my bicycle so we can move from the restaurant to a bar, my date laughs and says:

You did it again just now.

Did what just now?

You did it like that before when you locked your bike. Why do you do it like that?

I look down at myself, and I'm standing with bent legs and a hunched back, curved over with my hips pressed forward. And I can't remember when I started locking my bike like this. I can't remember when I started bending my whole lower body away from the street, each time I lock my bike. Do I do this every time? Have I done it for a long time? Do I do it on purpose? How long have I changed my body, scrunched myself together, made myself smaller without really noticing?

I don't manage to talk about anything else for the rest of the date. I talk about it all the time.

He says it's terrible that men slap women on the butt. Just walk up and do it.

I wave it off. It's not really about that. It's about the fact that I've changed myself. Once again, I've become someone I don't know.

It's not about the slap. It's about the consequence. It's about Ivan Pavlov and his dogs, about bells and electric shocks. It's about conditioned behavior. I've become a dog. Don't you understand that?

The date doesn't go so well.

I start to call my bicycle Pavlov.

When I go out to ride now, I try to remember to keep my legs straight and to bend my body into a ninety-degree angle. This is important. But there's always so much to remember.

Going Out

Oslo. I've walked all over Oslo. I've lived in Oslo for eight years. I've lived on the west side and on the east side, and I've mostly walked. On all kinds of streets and in all kinds of neighborhoods.

I've walked in red fluttering summer dresses. I've walked barefoot in sandals, barefoot without sandals. I've walked in jeans. I've walked in high heels and Doc Martens. I've walked in a hoodie, in a traditional Norwegian sweater knitted for a two-year-old that I use as a bolero, in Norwegian sweaters knitted for adults. I've walked in ankle-length linen pants and in outfits that I have to iron in the morning before I can wear them.

And in all kinds of streets, in all kinds of outfits, I'm asked how much I cost.

For half an hour, for an hour, for a night. What's my rate? Is my time, my body for sale?

The different instances have begun to blur together, but at the same time I can point to all the streets on the map and say, I was wearing this there, and still it happened. Almost all the brown women I know have experienced this. And it hasn't only happened once. Not like the time I was walking in The Square, on the side streets by Karl Johan. But like that time in Majorstua and Grünerløkka. In Akker Brygge. On the way out to H&M in the Oslo City mall. I've been asked by embarrassed men, by polite men, by men in cars with empty car seats in the backseat, by men in suits, by men in Hawaiian shirts, by men who apologize, who apologize again and again when I answer in Norwegian after they've asked me in English, and by men who get angry and slam me against their cars, press their faces against mine, and reject my refusal because it's not mine to give. Whores don't get to say no.

It's a cliché. It has happened often enough to become a cliché.

I didn't want to write about it. Didn't want to talk about it. I wanted to walk out the door. Wanted to hop on my bicycle. Wanted to take a taxi.

But I know most people don't know this happens. It isn't a used-up, recycled, regurgitated experience they just can't bear to talk about anymore. Not for most people.

And the man in the bar can't know all this when he asks if he can buy me a beer. He doesn't know that being bought evokes totally different connotations for me.

And I get angry at him because he doesn't understand. I get angry because my clichés are unfamiliar to him. And sometimes he experiences all my rage. This lone man in the bar gets to hear everything I didn't say to those other men in the streets, because I'm not alone in the bar, and I'm not afraid in the bar.

So, when this man in the bar assumes that we are standing on common ground, like two neutral bodies who can simply buy each other a beer, I get furious. And that's unfair. He knows as little about the men on Bogstadveien as my grandma knew about the ladies on the 17th of May.

I'm angry just the same. In those moments, I know my anger as well as I know the taste of my own spit.

I know it's unfair.

I want to break him.

I know I can't make him afraid, but I can make him feel small. I know we're all just children on the inside, and if I manage to bring his child to the surface, then I can best him, make him feel ashamed of himself. I can take revenge. I can laugh at him.

In these moments, I wonder where the impulse comes from. When did it happen? When did I become like this? Am I like this? I wonder if this is how the stereotype of the angry Black woman came about. Am I an angry Black woman now? When did I get so angry? Is this who I am now?

I don't laugh. I say, No thanks. Thanks just the same. I smile. I know it's unfair. I know it's unfair, and I'm not crazy. I seldom lose control.

Sometimes I try to turn it around. Sometimes I'm interested. Can I buy you a beer instead? Sometimes he says yes. Sometimes he says no. Maybe he says no because he saw it in my eyes before I smiled. Maybe he saw my anger and thought he would taste it in my spit if I took him home and stuck my tongue in his mouth.

But sometimes he says yes. And sometimes it's me who goes up to him at the bar. This is important.

Brownness for Sale

I have to confess that I don't really want to write this book. I'd rather write a book about vampires in outer space. When I was little, I wanted to be something I called triple A: astronaut-astronomer-archaeologist. I wanted to discover new planets, travel to them, and dig up old civilizations. And I always thought that all the mythological creatures we read about here on earth were actually beings from space who had visited us in the past.

I talk at conferences and demonstrations, to government agencies and institutions. I write theater. I stand on stages. I talk with politicians, teachers, students, journalists. I answer long emails and short Facebook messages. I write this book.

I'm afraid that my whole life has been reduced to the color of my skin. That I myself have played a willing part.

I'm afraid I've sold my brownness to the white public, and now I'm capitalizing on it. I'm afraid I'm brown first and foremost. Brown first, and everything else afterward.

Brown first, then daughter.

Brown first, then friend.

Brown first, then artist.

I'm probably most afraid that I won't be believed.

What happens when all my work is based on my own experiences?

I experience something. I document it. I pass it on.

I go around remembering things.

I note what they were wearing, what I was wearing, where we were, if it was raining.

I categorize things:

Did it happen because I'm queer?

Because I'm a woman? Because I'm brown?

Could it be a combination of all three?

Have I considered that maybe that person was just having a bad day?

Did it actually have anything to do with me?

I read research reports, statistics, histories, books.

I contextualize my experiences, recognizing the general framework.

And I ask people to trust me, to believe me.

How many stories do I have to collect before it's enough? How many witnesses do I have to call before it's confirmed? Before people are convinced?

I'm constantly aware that it's never been better to be a queer brown woman in Scandinavia than it is right now.

I know this. How grateful should I be?

I'm afraid we're regressing, progressing too slowly.

I'm ungrateful and impatient.

So I document.

And deep inside, I'm afraid it doesn't help. That what I do doesn't really matter.

The Stupidity of Youth

I choose to sit down next to another person of color on the bus. As if to compensate for my youthful stupidity. Sometimes I catch myself laughing out loud on the bus. I know this probably doesn't mean anything to anyone but me. I feel like I'm stalking men who look like my father, girls who look like my little sister. I break with Norwegian etiquette, with the rule that says you shouldn't sit in an empty seat right next to another passenger. I do it anyway, to appease my conscience.

Stockholm—Oslo—Copenhagen

A friend asks me if I liked Stockholm. He asks how I'd compare Stockholm to Oslo or Copenhagen.

I tell him Stockholm was liberating. That I'm beautiful in Stockholm. And not beautiful for a brown girl. Just beautiful. And even though I know I only surround myself with hipsters, with artists and members of the upper middle class, hanging out in bars around Södermalm, interacting with the cultural elite, even though I know all these things influence the situation, I still got to be just beautiful during the two months I lived there. Not exotic. The people who slept with me slept with me, not with the color of my skin.

I think, Fuck. Now I'm talking about it again.

My friend responds, That's the thing with Sweden: they're so politically correct they don't dare to say what they really think.

And even though I know he doesn't mean it, he says without skipping a beat that I'll always be a little exotic, that everybody thinks so.

It's just not something everybody says.

And maybe it's true people think like this. Maybe Oslo and Copenhagen are more liberating for the speaker because people aren't afraid to say what they think. And feel. And believe.

But it's very freeing for the receiver to recognize that the speaker can be a little bit afraid. You should be a little bit afraid. I'd really appreciate it if you'd think better of saying it. It costs me more than you realize to carry your thoughts about my body around in my body.

Stop

I experience moments when my body says, Stop. I'm done with this conversation. I'm never going to have this conversation again. I promise myself: this is the last time.

The most important conversation I've had about the N-word was with my own family. Many years after my brother tried the same thing.

I went to the library first. I searched online, found articles and history, and then I said, These are the things you're calling us. This is slavery and segregation. It's race theory and dehumanization. This is postcolonialism, linguistics, and ignorance. This is racism. Now they know it. Now they can't claim ignorance. Now it's all on them.

And almost no one in the family uses that word anymore. These conversations work. Sometimes they help. The educator wins.

Sometimes, of course, after too much aquavit on Christmas Eve, someone brings it up, saying, Come on, can't we . . . ? Why can't I . . . ?

But I don't need to take the conversation home anymore. Because I'm not alone. Mom stands up, Grandpa stands up, Grandma stands up, and they take the conversation on for me.

Our collective "we" strikes the idiocy down, so I can relax. I don't even need to open my mouth. Sometimes I lay my head down on the table, melodramatically, showing my frustration without saying a word. Or I go out and smoke a cigarette, knowing it will all be over when I come back.

Mass Effect

Eleven of us are sitting around a table drinking beer after a performance. We're in Copenhagen, but everyone around the table is Norwegian. I sit by a woman, a teacher.

She calls me *neger*.

My body seizes up. I inhale. Exhale. I wonder, Will I let it go on this particular evening? After all, I was just planning to stay for one beer. I have other places to be.

She uses the word on her way into another sentence. She says she has students who are *negrar*, like me, and could she tell me a sweet story about one of these students? This woman has students . . .

I speak up.

And the people around the table start regurgitating everything I've heard before. Everything we've all heard before. Is everything we do suddenly wrong now, or what?

The educator is activated.

I lay out the evidence. The history. I repeat myself. This is slavery and segregation. It's race theory and dehumanization. This is postcolonialism, linguistics, and ignorance. This is racism. I repeat it all without sounding shrill. In an inside voice. A voice without noise.

And she says, Oh. Everyone says, Oh. She hadn't thought about that. And she's going to think about it more. And next time she'll even think better of it.

I smile.

And then the tears come. She's ashamed.

I give her a hug, rub her hand.

And then she thanks me. And that's what makes my body really seize up.

She thanks me for working through this with her in such a calm and educational way. Because usually, when we talk about this, they get so angry, and it was really nice that you didn't. And maybe more people would understand if they did it like you, talking through it calmly, without being so aggressive. Sometimes it really takes just one conversation to change someone's heart, she says. Thank you so much.

She's happy I'm not like the others. I chew on that. I consider that she's grateful because I'm not angry.

I tell her that her gratitude means very little to me. That her tears don't help anyone, least of all me. I say this might be just one conversation for her, but I've had it well over a hundred times. I tell her I have to choke back my anger with my spit to have this conversation, again, in an inside voice. A calm voice, a voice without noise. For her sake. But it's not my fucking job to be sweet and educational with her. She's not my responsibility. It's her responsibility to seek out the information for herself. She could have easily googled it, instead of putting the responsibility on me, so I have to sit here making sure she's enlightened and well mannered.

And I advise her to do just that next time.

The mood around the table is tense. I think about the fact that this happened. This happened just now. And it doesn't bother me. It's not my problem. My body is relaxed. I chug my beer, say goodbye, and go.

I promise myself this was the last time. From here on out, I'm letting myself off the hook.

As I wander across the street, tipsy, I think about how this will free up a lot of time. I'll use the time to play Xbox.

African Time

I'm going on a date. I text her to let her know I'm running fifteen minutes late from work. I walk through the door of the restaurant, apologizing, and sit down. She smiles a dazzling, beautiful smile, and says, No problem, she had expected it, you know, *African time.*

I freeze. I look at her smile. I decide to let it go. I let it go because she's beautiful.

Later, when we are lying in her bed, her blonde hair spread out over my chest, I can't stop thinking about it. Because I let it pass, I can't let it go. Do I just keep quiet when it benefits me?

For the rest of our relationship, I keep watch over her words. I weigh them, follow along carefully. I've promised myself that the next time she says something like that, I'm going to say something back. I'm completely caught up in it. I'm focused on what she might say, and on what I will answer when she says it, and I don't actually listen to what she says when she talks to me.

She doesn't say anything like that again. I'm almost disappointed.

Pillow Talk

I'm in bed with a man who is telling a story about his first relationship. About the first time and the first love, about everything you didn't know then but know now, about everything you didn't know when you went through the first breakup. My body is relaxed, I listen, now and then I laugh. When he's finished with the story, he adds that it wasn't until he became an adult that he thought about the fact that she was adopted so late from India. Maybe that was why she clung to him so tightly.

My body freezes.

She was brown. She was brown, and I am brown. Is this a pattern? Is this his type? Or are we just two women in his life who happen to be brown, separated by twenty years?

I let it go.

She was brown, and that wasn't the point of the story. She was brown, and he didn't mention it before it was relevant, until the end. He is white, and I am brown, and I probably would have started the story with the fact that she was brown. Doesn't that mean I'm the one with the problem?

I talk about it, after all, all the time.

Low-Frequency Feelings

Writing this book makes me angry. I'm aware of it. I'm angry at my editor too, at the publisher, at myself, and at readers. I'm angry because it's all about finding a language that isn't didactic, that isn't aggressive, that isn't confrontational, that isn't moralizing. But it should be vulnerable. An open, searching, vulnerable language.

My editor and I go back and forth about how hard I can come off in the opening of the book because readers have to be able to get to know me before they notice my anger. She says my constant desire to quit could have a demoralizing effect, if I haven't given a good explanation as to why I decide to quit all the time. And she's right.

I write to her that it's fine by me if readers discover they don't like me. But it's not really about that. Not really.

It's about walking a fine line: showing how difficult this is, how deeply it impacts me, but without looking like a victim.

Without looking like I'm complaining. Or ungrateful. Or unsympathetic.

I'm afraid I don't have it in me anymore. This language that's supposed to humanize me. I'm afraid you'll read this text and decide what I'm writing about isn't important enough. I'm afraid

I'm speaking for people who aren't me, for a person who hasn't asked me to speak for them. I'm afraid it doesn't help. That I talk about the same thing again and again to no end. That I'm really only interested in myself.

I'm afraid we are regressing.

And then I get angry.

But you can't make people understand by scolding them. I know that. Guilt isn't productive. It's a low-frequency feeling.

A Little Man

I often dream about the same things. Things recur. When I was a child, I often dreamed about Carl Ivar Hagen, leader of the right-wing Progress Party from 1978 to 2016.

In the dream, Carl I. Hagen leans a ladder up against the wall of our house and crawls into my bedroom window, like Santa. He doesn't have presents with him, just a sack, and he stuffs me into it. He slings me on his back and climbs back down the ladder. He throws me into the bed of a pickup truck, drives me to the docks, and puts me into a container. He says he's going to send me back. I never arrive anywhere, just drift out onto the ocean.

When I was around ten years old, I saw Carl I. Hagen in the square in Sandefjord. He was standing there giving a speech. I clung tightly to Mom, but he wasn't as tall as I'd imagined.

Playing the Victim

It sounds like a costume I can put on and take off.

Cultural Capital

I call from Gardermoen airport outside Oslo to say that I'll be late to the meeting. They can start on the budget without me. I've been stopped by border control and won't make the train I'd planned to take.

When I get to the meeting, twenty minutes late, I apologize.

The leader of the meeting says he's never been stopped by border control.

I take a deep breath, look at him, and say, I get stopped all the time. It happens all the time.

He says they probably stop the prettiest girls.

Someone laughs.

I raise my hands to my face and rub my eyes, press my eyeballs into my cranium, exhale, and ask if they've started on the budget.

I let accounting distract me from the heavy mood that descended when I didn't laugh along. I let the numbers distract me from my anger because it was my lack of laughter and not his witty comment that ruined the mood. I look at the clock to figure out a good time to ask for a smoke break.

Traveling by Plane

I'm sitting at Gardermoen airport, on my way to Helsinki, where I'm going to give a lecture. The woman behind the desk says it's time for *priority boarding*, and those who have it can board first. I get up and go over to the scanner. A man in a suit puts his hand on my shoulder and says, Excuse me, but this is when people in first class get to check in first.

Yeah, I say. And just look at him.

Traveling by Train

I get on the train from Stockholm to Copenhagen. I put my baggage on the upper storage shelf. A woman leans over and says, Excuse me, but these are reserved seats.

I look at her.

She says, This is first class.

Yeah, I say. I just keep looking at her.

The Arts and Culture Center
for Nynorsk

It's evening on Rosenkrantz's gate, and we're doing lighting for a performance that will premiere in a few days. I go outside, lean against the pillars, and smoke a cigarette.

A man comes walking along. He's walking slowly and looking around. He looks at his mobile phone, looks around again. He stops and looks through the windowpane in the door, into the light. He looks around, and then he looks at me.

I say, Hi? in Norwegian.

He says, No thank you. No, no, no, thank you, in English.

He hurries away.

I'm rubbing my face when I enter the foyer.

My colleague looks at me.

I tell him what just happened.

Poor guy, he says, and chuckles. It must be scary to come from a small village into Oslo and not know any better. He was probably scared to death.

Poor guy. I consider that.

I check to see if I have space to accommodate his fear in my body.

I don't.

I go out and smoke another cigarette. I pull the smoke down deep in my belly.

Tequila

I call a friend to tell her I'm going to write this story. But I can't remember: Did the man at the bar call me darkie when I refused to give him my number? That time we had agreed to drink beer but drank tequila instead?

She gets quiet.

No. He called you nigger.

Thanks, I say. Thanks for remembering.

Do I make things easier on myself? What have I forgotten? What does my body refuse to bear?

My heart rate goes up when I think I might be misremembering. How is anyone supposed to believe me if I misremember?

Was that what he said? What I said? What she said? Where were we? What was I wearing? Was it snowing?

Blabbermouth

My friend's boyfriend asks me for advice. We're in the sixth grade, standing on the playground. It's all-school recess. He asks about making out and kissing and bases. About things he wants to try with her. He asks me about fingering.

I've been in love with his girlfriend for almost a year, and I'm jealous. I'm blindingly jealous of him, the one who gets to be with her, who gets to say out loud that he's in love with her.

I call him a gross pervert.

He responds with Fat fucking nigger whore.

When I walk through the door at home I start to cry. Mom is furious. She calls his parents.

The next day at school everyone says I'm a blabbermouth. That I blabbed to my mom. That I said something nasty to him first and couldn't handle something ugly being thrown back at me. I'm unable to explain to them that it's not the same thing.

My friend is mad at her boyfriend. She takes my side.

Did I get what I wanted?

I decide never to tell my mom anything ever again.

Gratitude

We do a round of introductions at the board meeting. I say my name and tell them I'm here to talk about working with children and Nynorsk, one of two standard written languages in Norway, officially spoken by a minority of Norwegians (the language I'm using to write this book). A woman on the board turns toward me and says, Don't you mean slang?

Slang? I ask.

Yeah, you know, slang. Isn't that you?

Youth, First

I was fourteen years old the first time I gave my voice away.

A friend of a friend of my mom's is going to make a documentary series for television about adolescents with minority backgrounds. I get a video camera and six months. I return cassettes filled with footage regularly, have conversations about what's important. I feel important. Everything I have to say is important. She believes me.

My footage will be edited down to a little video.

I hand over the last cassette and wait.

In the meantime, I'm confirmed by the Norwegian Humanist Association.

I travel to Oslo to watch the film. The girl in the film is a stranger. I don't recognize myself. It was definitely me. It was me in the film, but the story wasn't mine. The girl in the film came across as a fucking victim.

The director had decided what was important.

I didn't know how brown I was until I experienced someone else editing me together. When I saw the film, it seemed like I set myself apart, represented myself as more isolated than I actually felt. It seemed like the girl in the film cried an awful lot. Like she was whiny and complained and felt really sorry for herself.

Later, I concluded that it was because the film was about being brown, first and foremost. Brown first, and then maybe an adolescent.

The director asked me what I thought, and I didn't say anything. And because I didn't say anything, she couldn't know I hated the film. That it made my eyes burn and seize up on the train ride home.

I don't remember the content of the film itself very clearly. That isn't important. It was never broadcast.

I promised myself I would never give my voice away again.

New Sweater

I buy myself a new sweater that's a bit too expensive and imagine that the lady on the train paid for it. I deserve money for this. It feels good to be able to use her for something, something other than just sitting and chewing on her comments all the way from Stockholm to Copenhagen. I sat ramrod straight the whole trip, working on some document or other on my laptop instead of doing what I'd normally do (watch *Grey's Anatomy*) just in case she peeked over her seat. I did it so she would understand that I'm important. Important enough to be able to pay the extra fucking 300 kroner for a first-class ticket, which she just assumed I didn't have.

I put the sweater on, look at myself in the mirror, and feel irritated. I think about this lady every time I wear it now. I'd hoped that once I put her down in words, I could let her go. Now I carry her around in my body, and on it.

Loop

I remind myself that I sometimes have a loud, piercing laugh that fills the entire room. That drowns everyone else out. That makes me gasp for air.

And sometimes I laugh until I'm hoarse. People often say I laugh just like Marge Simpson. I snort when somebody says something funny. I am also this.

He Hit First

A friend and I are sitting on a bench on Karl Johan, leaning up against each other. We've toasted with champagne one too many times, and we're smashed. We just opened an exhibition about the children of incarcerated parents, and we did it without crying. So now we're good and drunk, sitting on a bench on Karl Johan. And we're crying.

A group of men in their early twenties comes along, asking if we'd like to join them for an afterparty. I say, Thanks anyway, boys, have a nice party.

One of them refuses to give up. He insists that it will be the best party, the best, and they have everything we need, and they'll pay for the taxi.

Can't you see we're sitting here crying and minding our own business? I say. Don't you see that she's crying? Can't you just leave us alone?

He tosses Fucking darkie over his shoulder and follows after his friends, who've already given up.

My friend asks, What the fuck did he say?

Let it go, I say, just let it go.

She gets up from the bench and runs after him. She shouts after him, and when he turns around, she hits him in the face with a closed fist.

58

One of his friends—this happens so fast—turns around and punches her down. She falls to the ground. She doesn't get up. I realize I'm still standing by the bench. She's been knocked down, she's lying alone, in the middle of the street. The men look at each other, frightened. They look at her lying there and run. By the time I walk over, several people have gathered around. She wakes up. They say they saw it. They can call the police. One of them is a nurse, Get her to the emergency room.

She's still furious at the emergency room. She doesn't want to wait in line. She wants to go out into the streets and find them, knock them down, all of them. She wants to knock them down for me.

We don't call the police. She hit first.

He hit first, she says.

Words aren't violence, I say, and I almost believe it.

I try to calm her down.

I tell her this happens all the time.

She doesn't calm down.

The Rope

Remembering is the most difficult thing. I have to act as my own witness all the time.

The Nazis are marching in the streets. In Kristiansand. In Stockholm.

In Copenhagen as well, but there's only two of them. I read the article in the paper and laugh.

Nazi demonstration in Copenhagen, two participants. One Dane and one Swede. Where's the Norwegian? The leader of the demonstration didn't even show up. He went to Kristiania to drink beer instead, together with other Nazis who didn't show up. And they got kicked out.

They're marching in America. I'm not laughing. The rhetoric is brutal. I watch the VICE documentary about Charlottesville, where journalist Elle Reeve interviews extreme right organizers. They say they're inspired by the Nordic Resistance Movement, a National Socialist organization. The same guys who marched in Kristiansand, less than two weeks before Heather Heyer was run down by a car. In the interview, they say we're so good at organizing in Scandinavia. Our movements are built on brotherhood and solidarity.

I think, We export fish, Ibsen, and neo-Nazism. Hate is the new oil.

People are in shock when they march in Kristiansand. People are furious. My Facebook feed overflows.

Where did they come from?
Didn't they disappear after Benjamin Hermansen was murdered by the Boot Boys in 2001?

Some of us know they've been here the whole time. They've just grown their hair out.
We went to the same parties in middle school. For the most part, you learned to avoid them. If Vigrid was in the kitchen, then you went into the living room. If they came into the living room, you took your beer out into the garden. We'd all known each other since preschool. Everybody knew somebody's brother.
If you didn't provoke them, everything would be fine. We must all learn to avoid things. We can't not invite them to the party. We're all friends here.

I got beaten up when I was fourteen.
This is the most difficult thing. I remember nothing. I remember a kick to the back.
Do I remember a kick to the back? Running shoes? Work boots? Big dress shoes?
I think I remember a kick to the back.
I remember I was about to throw up, that I lost my balance, fell against the toilet seat, got a lump on my head.

After that, I don't remember anything. And since I know the kick to my back happened after my head hit the toilet seat, it seems I can't remember that either. What I remember is the bruise.

How can I talk about something I don't remember?

I remember I woke up in my own bed and thought I wasn't supposed to have slept there that night. I'd lied, saying I was going to sleep at a friend's house.

I remember Mom. She's sitting on a chair by the bed, sleeping with her head resting on my duvet. I turn over. My body aches. She sees I'm awake, and she's not angry. She cries.

I remember I walk into the bathroom and see the bruises along my ribs. The lump on my head. I feel my back is sore.

I can't be my own witness. This is probably the most difficult thing. They're friendly at the police station. I get a glass of water. The light is bright. My stepfather is there.

We agree that Mom is too emotional.

I can't help them. I can't help myself. A friend called her brother. A neighbor lady called the police.

I'm told I was dragged out onto the courtyard.

Let's tie her legs up to the car and drag her along the road. Let's see how much a *neger* can take.

It went far enough that someone brought out a rope.

I remember I felt bad for the policeman who tried to understand the details, any kind of detail, when he asked if I remembered the car, or the tattoos, or how many people there were, or if they had blond or brown or red hair, anything at all.

He gets frustrated with me. I understand why. But I don't understand how serious it is. I don't divulge the names of people at the party. I'm afraid they'll find out how we got alcohol. I'm afraid my friends will get in trouble.

I don't want to be a blabbermouth.

I don't want to lie, either. I don't remember anything.

I decide it wasn't a real trauma because I can't remember anything.

Maybe it came about later, when some of my friends were more worried about me keeping quiet than about whether or not I was OK. Because it was their brother's friends, or people we went to kindergarten with, and, Yeah, it went too far, but you puked all over the bathroom, and people were angry because they had to clean up your puke.

You can't hold your alcohol.

The Nazis are marching in the streets, and I go to bed. I decide yet again to quit. I decide to write a vampire novel. I have lists of ideas. How much sunlight is there in outer space? Will vampires be equally affected by different types of stars? Vampires don't need oxygen.

I think about Benjamin. Before Benjamin and after Benjamin. I realize it happened so long ago that everyone is out of prison again. The people who killed him have gotten out, have done their time.

I don't know what they look like. Maybe I've held a door open for one of them on the way into a store? Have we sat together on the bus?

They were adults when they did it, but now I'm older than they were when they did it.

I always felt I'd be exploiting something I didn't have a right to if I grieved Benjamin too much.

The people who knew him best also went to the Center for Anti-racism's summer camp. Mom would eventually send us there every summer, but 2001 was the first time we attended on our own. We could write on the memorial they had dedicated to him.

I felt it wasn't my loss to grieve.

But they were so warm. They included me in the grieving process. They said it was a shared grief. It was collective. They were also children, adolescents, with such big hearts. They called him Benny, Baloo. I felt like a bloodsucker.

I always feel like a bloodsucker when I talk about the racist murder of a fifteen-year-old boy who was Norwegian but brown.

Who was killed because he looked like my brother.

We always got extra attention: Did you know him? Were you friends? Did he know your brother? They look alike, actually, in the picture in the papers. Were they related?

When Benjamin was stabbed to death, he was fifteen, and I was twelve.

When they brought my rope out, I was fourteen.

It's my rope now, even if I don't remember it. From the moment they brought it out, the ownership of the rope shifted from the one who was going to tie it around my legs to me.

No. The rope became mine the moment someone told me about it. Because I don't remember it.

How can you own something you don't remember?

When the Nazis storm Stockholm Pride, everyone is shocked and asks where they came from.

They've been here the whole time.

I want to shout it out into my echo chamber, which resounds with shock and disbelief.

They've been here the whole fucking time.

Why don't they know this? Haven't I told you all this? Is it because I don't talk about it enough? Because I talk about it all the time.

Mania

I'm obsessed with the details. I have to remember everything. I take a notebook with me everywhere, write things down.

Source Critique

Am I a trustworthy source? Do I become more or less trustworthy if I insist upon it?

Mom's Memory

In 1989, when my mom moved from Bodø to Oslo together with me and my brother, she went to an apartment showing. She got the apartment.

A few days later, she dropped by to sign the contract and get the keys.

We are with her. Me and my brother. I'm sitting in the stroller. He's standing beside it. We are one and three years old.

The man opens the door and stares at us. What's this? he asks Mom.

These are my children, she says. I told you I have two children.

I don't rent to trash. Not to filthy rats, he says, and slams the door in our faces.

I don't remember this. I was only one. Just the same, I can tell you the color of the walls: gray. The color of the door: white. How the man looked: he had dark-blond hair.

I don't remember it. But I see it clearly before me just the same.

Mom has told me this story many times. The story comes up a lot.

I invented the hallway, the color of the door, and the man's hair color myself, and I can't hear the man's words without seeing the color of the slammed door.

I carry this memory, but it isn't mine. Just the same, I own it.
I remember being told about it.
Trash. Filthy rats.

I often wonder what the point is. Why do I have to know this,
carry this?

Did Mom have less to carry after she shared the burden?

I remember I felt so indignant. I remember I asked Mom why
she didn't call the police. I remember I thought this man didn't
have the right to do that to my mom. Somebody did this to my
mom. And I remember I was disappointed in Mom because she
didn't do anything. I imagined her knocking on the door again
and spitting on him. He hit first, and Mom hit back. But words
aren't violence.

She got help to find another apartment from someone who
worked at the Center for Anti-racism. Nothing could be done
about the apartment she'd been promised.

The way we were treated wasn't illegal in Norway until 2003.

This story has become part of my memory. I realized that even
though the white people at home loved me, other white people
could still think I was dirty. Some kind of trash. A filthy rat.

Proximity to whiteness has meant that when I entered a room, I
generally assumed the white people in that room would love me,
not think of me as trash. I often wonder what it would feel like
to experience a door slammed in my face, without also having
grown up with white people who pushed me on the swings, put
Band-Aids on my scratches, dressed me in pajamas, and sang
me to sleep.

Red

While we're getting dressed, the man at whose home I won't be spending the night after all says his mom was really happy when he told her about me.

How does his mother know who I am? I pause.

Why was she happy?

She votes socialist, he answers.

What does that have to do with anything?

Oh, she's really anti-racist, so she's always wanted me to . . . you know . . . so she's proud now. She's told her friends and stuff.

Apolitical

A friend tells another friend that he doesn't care about politics.

There are people out there who don't want me to exist. What a fucking nauseous privilege, to allow yourself not to care about politics. How dare you not care?

I shout in his face. The party goes totally silent. Only the music keeps playing.

Later we're standing out on the balcony. I say I'm sorry. I tell him I don't always recycle. And I throw my cigarette butts down on the street. Even though I know that the planet is being destroyed. I know it.

Someone Else's Brother

When a fourteen-year-old boy puts his dirty shoes on the tram seat, I get irritated. I wonder if I'm more irritated with him than I would be with a boy without brown skin.

I realize I'm disproportionately annoyed with him because I'm blaming him for the fact that the lady on the train doesn't believe I can sit in first class.

I'm almost more annoyed with him than I was with her.

I think about all the times I told my brother it was no wonder he always got stopped by the police, since he walked around with his pants sagging. That if he'd just dress better, he wouldn't get so much crap. And he answered back, You're fucking white, you know.

My guilty conscience rears its head. I realize I still haven't called my brother to apologize.

I sit down next to the boy and smile at him. The lady on the train isn't a burden he should have to carry. He should get by without having to carry my self-disparagement as well.

What I really want to do is rub the boy's arm and give him a hug. I keep my hands folded in my lap to stop myself from reaching out to him.

You're on the Wrong Train, Sir

A man comes running onto the train, at the last second. He's out of breath and asks loudly if it's the train to Karlstad. The train pulls away from the station. He looks out the window at the platform and asks, in an even louder voice, Is this the train to Karlstad? I lean out into the aisle and tell him, Yes, this train goes to Stockholm, and I think it stops in Karlstad on the way.

He takes a seat, relieved, pulls off his jacket, is sweaty underneath.

I consider telling him that these are assigned seats but change my mind. I don't want to assume he doesn't belong in first class, even though that's exactly what I just assumed.

I listen to some music.

The conductor comes by, and I turn the music off. She stops beside him, looks at his ticket, and says in English, You're on the wrong train, sir.

He jumps up, answering her in Norwegian, Wrong train? Wrong train? They said it was the right train. Am I on the wrong train?

She backs up, responding in English again, I need you to calm down, or I will have to call security.

He holds his hands up, warily, with palms turned toward her, and says in a quieter voice, I'm not trying to be difficult, but can you tell me if I'm on the train to Karlstad?

Yes, she says in Swedish, You're on the train to Karlstad, but you're in the wrong car. This is first class, and you can't sit here. If you can't calm down, then you can't ride the train at all. You'll have to get off at the next station.

But I *am* calm, he says, and sighs in frustration.

Switching to English again, she says, Sir, calm down. You are being very loud, very aggressive. I will call security.

She says this very loudly.

Sorry, *unnskyld*, sorry, he answers.

I think to myself, I should turn around and say that he's not the one being aggressive. She's the one being difficult and loud. He isn't threatening, he isn't loud, he sounds like my father. He rolls his *r*'s just like my father. He has the same skin color as my father.

I had decided not to write about Dad in this book.

While I sit here considering whether I should defend the man on the train, he slips his arm back into his jacket and says in Norwegian, Sorry, sorry, I wasn't trying to be aggressive. Then, switching back and forth between English and Norwegian, Sorry. I didn't mean to scare you. I will find my seat. *Ha en fin dag.* Have a nice day, ma'am.

He walks toward the back of the train.

The woman comes up to me, smiling. I think, I should say something to you. I should ask you if you would threaten to call security if a white man stood up in a panic, or if you would've pasted on a service smile, explaining that it was just a misunderstanding. I should tell her it wasn't his problem but hers, that she should really take a good look at herself.

And you could have fucking answered him in Swedish. Why did you have to speak English? Have you thought about that, or . . . ?

But I don't say anything to her. I give her my ticket, she says thanks, and moves on.

Now that she's done checking the tickets in our car, she goes on to the next car.

I feel sick. Nausea rises up in my body. It starts in my diaphragm. I think maybe it's motion sickness, but I know very well it isn't. It's shame.

It would have been so easy for me to defend him. I could have stood up for him. I chose not to, and in this moment, I realize I wouldn't have stood up for my own father either.

If I didn't know him, I wouldn't stand up to defend my own father.

I had decided not to write about Dad in this book.

It's a short book, part of a series, limited in terms of length. My father deserves more than being reduced to an episode. To a few short anecdotes. I thought, My father has been so reduced by society, he can be spared being reduced in this book.

My father is an elegant man who likes to match his socks with his hat, tie, and suit jacket. His laughter can drown out everything else in the room. Sometimes he laughs hoarsely, like Marge Simpson. He hates that I smoke, but he loves that it means I come down to smoke an evening cigarette before going to bed because then he can convince me to stay up with him, to have a cup of tea and a bite to eat.

I write to Dad on Messenger, tell him I'm considering writing about him in my book.

He answers, Hmmmmmmmmm, with a laughing face emoji.

I write that I promise to let him read it before I submit it, so he can tell me whether or not it's OK.

He answers: It's all OK by me. This is your story, I'm happy to help.

With four emojis. I don't need to remember this. I have digital evidence. My dad is a man who loves to use emojis.

He's also an immigrant felon.

Black man, criminal past.

Muslim.

How do you fight, protect yourself against racist stereotypes, when your dad is one of them?

My father is a multifaceted person, a man with all kinds of positive and negative personality traits. He matches his socks and tie. He uses emojis. But people often don't remember this if they've heard about his rap sheet.

And this book doesn't have room for the whole person. This book only has room for fragments.

So, I'd come to the decision not to write about Dad.

But in this moment, when I see the man walk toward the back of the train, slumped over, with no one having defended him, I realize I wouldn't have defended my own father.

And I've written a book that spends a good amount of time and energy asking people to defend me.

I can blame my failure to defend the man on the train on the fact that I never know whether helping will escalate or deescalate the situation. But that wasn't why.

It's because I don't know if I can stand to carry the discomfort. The discomfort of involving myself in an injustice that doesn't directly impact me. The anxious feeling that I might also be regarded as difficult. I have enough shit to deal with as it is.

But the point isn't to resolve the situation. It's highly unlikely that a single comment would convince the SJ-conductor to lose her bigotry.

The point is to reassure the man that he's not being aggressive, he's not the one being difficult. That he isn't threatening, even though she perceives him that way. That I know he isn't automatically dangerous just by virtue of the way he looks.

The train crosses the border between Norway and Sweden, and the Swedish landscape glides by. The nausea doesn't go away. I go get myself a cup of coffee.

The man is standing in the restaurant car. He's standing right in front of me in the line for the coffee machine.

I stare at him, almost reaching out my hand to tap his shoulder. He turns around and looks at me.

I don't say anything. He walks away.

I told myself I didn't want to write about Dad in this book because I wanted to protect him. But really, I wanted to protect myself.

I remember very well why I didn't like the documentary series from when I was fourteen. I lied when I wrote about it earlier. I hated the film because—in addition to all the crying and all the other relevant stuff—I said out loud on film that my dad had been in prison.

It was a slip of the tongue.

When I was fifteen and participating in a youth-in-politics debate, an opposing debater from the right-wing Progress Party Youth Association said, It isn't strange that Camara is a member of the Socialist Youth because they want open immigration, and she just wants to bring more of her criminal immigrant family members to Norway. Did you all know that her father is one of them?

And in that moment, I believed him. I bought his claim about my dad. On stage during the debate, I said I didn't have anything to do with him. That we didn't keep in contact, my dad and me. I lied again, so they would think I was good enough. So they would trust me.

I quit party politics for youth after that.

I had reduced my dad to the absent Black father stereotype. And by not naming him in this book, I did it again.

He hasn't been absent. He's never been only one thing. But there isn't space for all the things he is, and all the things that I am too, in this book.

I'm also a liar. Just the same, I ask my readers to trust me.

I know how difficult it is to defend the people around you. I often make mistakes. All the time. Just the same, I ask you not to quit. Even though I consider quitting all the time.

Avalanche

Someone says, That's not what happened. That's not what I said. It wasn't snowing.

Did I get everything wrong?

I ask, Is this the first time you've thought about it since you said it?

What does it matter? Are you allowed to let it go, are you allowed to forget, because you don't have to carry it around in your body later? Because you get to leave the conversation?

Or have I thought about it so much that the thoughts have taken over my memory? Did I get it right? Have you forgotten? Have I forgotten? Wasn't it snowing?

Is that important?

National Costume II

I've been told not to raise my hand so often in class. Give the other children a chance to answer as well.

Did I think that was why the woman with the umbrella hit me? Because I was showing off? Because I took up too much space?

Was that why I didn't say anything? Because I was afraid that the adults would tell me I talk too much again?

I try to remember the first time I told an adult about it. How long did I keep quiet?

Didn't I understand right away why she hit me?

She had an umbrella, but I don't remember if it was raining. Would she have an umbrella with her if it wasn't raining?

I check the weather for the 17th of May 1995 in Sandefjord in Vestfold at Yr.no.

Rainfall: one millimeter. It wasn't raining. What does that mean?

It rained on the 17th of May 1997. Was I older?

No. If that were the case, the dress wouldn't have fit me.

Did she maybe have a cane and not an umbrella?

Is the object she hit me with more important than the hit?

I call Grandma and ask if she remembers when I told her about it.

She remembers the event, but she doesn't remember when she heard about it.

I call Mom and read what I've written.

She says she remembers me telling her about it the next weekend.

I ask her when and whether it was at the breakfast table.

She says it's almost impossible for her to remember everything that happened, when it happened, where it happened. So much has happened.

Mom Is a Superhero

Because I already have Mom on the phone, I also read the story about my rope. Mom tells me that *she* called the police. That my friend called her brother, and when he arrived, they had to look for me, and he finally found me dumped in the snow on the edge of the ditch, behind the abandoned greenhouse. They thought I was going to freeze to death. The police might have been alerted by others, but she had also called the police. And child welfare. She had called everyone. And she hadn't told me all the details because she thought it might make things worse.

I apologize for thinking she'd been too emotional.

Your Silence Will Not Save You

The personal is political.

Can we change society by witnessing?

I want facts.

How many stories do we need? How many stories is enough?

Will a hashtag help?

Most of the things that happen to me aren't illegal. And I don't really think they should be.

Like I said, I often decide to stop. Stop talking about it. Stop writing things down. Change careers. Triple A, FTW.

Remove the burden of proof from myself.

At the same time, I know these things won't stop.

I sometimes doubt that it helps to talk about it, but I know for sure it doesn't help to keep quiet. Keeping quiet helps no one.

Your silence will not protect you. It won't save you.

It's not an alternative.

I haven't quit yet.

The educator is still activated.

But I'll let this go for now. Now that I've put these stories down on paper, the paper can carry the memories for me, the book can be the witness, whether it matters or not.

You can carry this book in your bag. Maybe that's what I want. That we carry this together.

Epilogue

I call my brother . . .

Translator's Note and Acknowledgments

OLIVIA NOBLE GUNN

A colleague gave me a copy of *Eg snakkar om det heile tida* (*I Talk about It All the Time*) (2018) at an academic conference in 2019. Thank you, Ellen Rees. Twenty or so pages in, I knew I wanted to teach the book in "Sexuality in Scandinavia," one of my undergraduate courses at the University of Washington. Goals for this course include beginning to unlearn truisms about history and the nature of progress and considering how and why sexuality is about everything, including place, class, religion, race, politics, and community. Camara Lundestad Joof's book was a great fit, so I took the liberty of translating excerpts to assign. Although I was careful to share only a small part, I felt uneasy. Would the author be okay with this? I decided to email her. Would she give me permission to continue sharing the already translated sections? Would she be okay with me translating the entire text? Joof responded with surprise and generosity. She hadn't imagined her book finding an audience at a university in the United States. We met online to discuss next steps, and then I invited her to take part in "Transcultural Approaches to Europe," a lecture series hosted by the Simpson Center for the Humanities and organized by the Departments of Scandinavian Studies, French and Italian, and German Studies at UW–Seattle.

Much has happened since that first online meeting. Perhaps most significantly, Joof became playwright in residence at the National Theatre in Oslo. In April 2022, she visited Seattle to take part in the lecture series at UW. She also attended a staged reading of her most recent work at the time, *De må føde oss eller pule oss for å elske oss* (*They Must Birth Us or Fuck Us to Love Us*) (2021), at the National Nordic Museum. Thank you to all the organizers, hosts, participants, and artists, including Emnet Kebreab, Leslie Anderson, Karoliina Kuisma, Jason Groves, Maya Smith, Kye Terrasi, Seattle Rep, Nabra Nelson, Nike Imoru, the School of Drama, Jasmine Mahmoud, Nikki Yeboah, Chinelo Okpala, Amber Walker, Esther Okech, and Amanda Rountree. Shortly thereafter, I was awarded sabbatical leave during the fall and winter of 2022–23. I spent that winter in Oslo, supported by a fellowship award from the American-Scandinavian Foundation. This meant that I had the great pleasure of attending *Samtaler med bror* (*Conversations with My Brother*) (2022), the second production from Joof's tenure as playwright in residence.

The brother(s) in *Samtaler med bror*—either one man split into three, or three men—both are and aren't the same brother that we hear about, but do not meet, in *I Talk about It All the Time*. One big difference between these works is that the former is fiction. Dramatic fiction gives Joof more room to play, to reimagine, to change the storyline. And this relieves some (certainly not all) of the palpable pressure in *I Talk about It All the Time*: the pressure to be believable; to back up memories with evidence; to wrestle with the possibility of misremembering, especially when your subject is racism and the majority white audience is likely looking for reasons to doubt and discredit, for reasons to believe that it can't be so bad because "we" are good.

Despite any liberties that fiction might provide, the brother(s) on stage and the brother named in the opening and closing pages of *I Talk about It All the Time* have things in common. They all figure longing for familial repair and for safer spaces for Black and brown Norwegians, somewhere just beyond the gazes and demands of white people. They sometimes embody Joof's fantastic and terrible talent for taking herself to task as well as her constant search for reprieve, a moment in which she might get things right, catch a break, feel believed. In *I Talk about It All the Time*, the majority white audience gets a lot of Joof's time and energy, her admonitions, and her generosity. In *Samtaler med bror*, we are more directly critiqued and ignored. Joof even leaves us alone in the theater for a while, with the lights up. We get to stare at one another while the brother(s) and sister(s) have an offstage dance party we aren't invited to. Joof's authorship offers us a challenge: Carry some of the burden, stop demanding so much emotional and educational labor from others, take people's lived and professional expertise seriously, know when to mind your own business, take yourself to task, give yourself a break. And when you fuck up, find a way to move on and do better.

I have been translating *I Talk about It All the Time* since I received the book as a gift in 2019. I have moved back and forth between the source text and my translation, reading and rereading, continually revising. Thank you, Amanda Doxtater, Elizabeth DeNoma, Maxine Savage, Elizabeth Stang, and Thea Lund for helping me think about and workshop the manuscript. One of the biggest challenges involved illustrating the divergence and overlap of racist, anti-Black language in Norway and the United States. In the early days of sharing with students, I translated

the Norwegian N-word as *Negro* and rendered the American
N-word as *n******. I included a footnote stating that this was
my choice. Students were welcome to ask me about my motiva-
tions and about the imprecision and ethical dilemmas involved.
Thanks are due to my students in "Sexuality in Scandinavia,"
especially those who dared to ask. The biggest problem with my
choice is that, while related, the Norwegian N-word and the term
Negro are not simply equivalent. They have different histories of
usage, rejection, and reclamation. In the end, I decided to leave
all the N-words in their original form, which already evokes the
abovementioned divergence and overlap, in my estimation.

I received Joof's book as a gift. Most of all, I want to thank her
for writing it and for her generosity in allowing me to translate
it. I hope readers will receive this translation as a gift, a challenge,
an opportunity to recognize transnational solidarities, to work
toward being, in Gayatri Chakravorty Spivak's words, "unaccusing" *and* "unexcusing," toward building other worlds even as we
are stuck in this one.[1]

Note

1. Gayatri Chakravorty Spivak, *A Critique of Postcolonial Reason:
Toward a History of the Vanishing Present* (Cambridge, MA: Harvard
University Press, 1999), 81. Spivak's entire phrase, a description of
the deconstructive mode, is "unaccusing, unexcusing, attentive, situa-
tionally productive through dismantling."

CAMARA LUNDESTAD JOOF is a Norwegian Gambian performance artist, playwright, and author. From 2020 to 2024, she was playwright in residence at the Norwegian National Theatre and had her first premiere there in 2021 with *De må føde oss eller pule oss for å elske oss* (*They Must Birth Us or Fuck Us to Love Us*). The script won the Hedda Award for Best Stage Text and was nominated for the National Ibsen Award of 2022. Her first book, *I Talk about It All the Time* (*Eg snakkar om det heile tida*, 2018), is an autobiographical essay on racism in Scandinavia. It has become part of the high school curriculum in Norway and is being taught at universities in Norway, Sweden, and the United States. It was nominated for the Norwegian Library Award in 2022. Beginning in 2024, Joof is the artistic director of Dramatikkens Hus (The Norwegian Centre for New Playwriting, or NCNP), the national development and resource center for new dramatic writing.

Maria Gossé

OLIVIA NOBLE GUNN
is an associate professor
and the Sverre Arestad
Endowed Chair in
Norwegian Studies
in the Department of
Scandinavian Studies
at the University of
Washington, Seattle.
Her research and teach-
ing interests include
comparative literature,
Norwegian literature and

culture after 1880, the classed and racialized history of the
family and child, feminism, queer theory, and theater and
performance studies. She is motivated by big questions about
innocence, propriety, and the limits of thinking and living.
First and foremost an Ibsen scholar, Gunn is the author of
*Empty Nurseries, Queer Occupants: Reproduction and the Future
in Ibsen's Late Plays* (2020). She is currently working on a book
on the question of progress in North American Ibsen adapta-
tions in the twenty-first century.

MONICA L. MILLER is a professor of Africana studies at Barnard College, Columbia University. A specialist in contemporary African American and Afrodiasporic literature and cultural studies, she is the author of the book *Slaves to Fashion: Black Dandyism and the Styling of Black Diasporic Identity* (2009). She is a frequent commentator in the media and arts worlds. Miller teaches and writes about Black literature, art, and performance; fashion cultures; and contemporary Black European culture and politics. A grantee from the Andrew W. Mellon Foundation, the Schomburg Center for Research in Black Culture, and the Institute for Scholars and Citizens, she is currently at work on a book project that considers cultural production by the emerging Black community in Sweden and its connection to Afrodiasporic identity formation and cultural/political movements.

NANA OSEI-KOFI is a professor emerita of women, gender, and sexuality in the School of Language, Culture, and Society at Oregon State University. As a critical feminist scholar, her research employs two lines of inquiry centered on justice and the politics of difference. One line of inquiry focuses on structural shifts in higher education in the service of equity and access through curriculum transformation, change leadership, and faculty development. Osei-Kofi's latest book in this area (coedited with Bradley Boovy and Kali Furman) is *Transformative Approaches to Social Justice Education: Equity and Access in the College Classroom* (2012). Her other line of inquiry centers on the experiences and conditions faced by people of African descent in Europe generally, and Sweden specifically, which is the subject of her forthcoming book.